AMAZING
Plants and Animals

Multilevel Nonfiction Book

Lakeshore Learning Materials
2695 E. Dominguez Street
Carson, CA 90895
www.lakeshorelearning.com
Made in China

ISBN 978-1-59746-058-3

Table of Contents

Amazing Plants and Animals

A Very Cold Place

Imagine that you are at the North Pole. You have no clothes and no shelter. All you can see for miles around is snow and ice. The wind is freezing cold, and there is no food. Will you be able to stay alive?

Of course you will, because you are a polar bear! You have thick fur and plenty of fat to keep you warm. You know how to hunt for seals and other food. In fact, you are well suited to live in your frozen world. A scientist would say that you have **adapted**, or changed, to fit your environment.

What Is an Environment?

An **environment** is the natural place where plants and animals live. Earth has many different environments, such as polar regions, rain forests, and deserts. Every environment is different. Each one is home to a unique set of plants and animals.

What Do Plants and Animals Need?

No matter where they live, all plants and animals need certain things to survive. They must have food, water, and **oxygen**. They must not be too hot or too cold. They must protect themselves from any animals that want to eat them. And they must **reproduce**. A living thing reproduces by making another plant or animal like itself. A plant makes seeds that grow into the same kind of plant. Animals have babies that grow up to be just like their parents.

Why Do Living Things Adapt?

Depending on the environment, some of these needs might be easy or hard to meet. For example, there is plenty of freshwater in wetlands and rain forests. But in deserts and grasslands, water is hard to find. To get what they need, plants and animals must adapt to their environments. Each living thing adapts in unique ways. As you will learn in this book, some of these adaptations are truly amazing!

Deserts

Deserts are very dry places. Most deserts get less than 10 inches of rain each year. There is one desert where no rain has fallen for hundreds of years! Deserts often have extreme temperatures, too. It can be burning hot during the day and freezing cold that same night.

At first glance, the desert looks empty. You do not see many animals moving around. There are a few plants, but they look dry and dead. It is hard to believe that the desert is full of amazing living things!

Using Every Drop

Let's look a little closer. See that rock? It's really a plant! It is called a stone plant. A stone plant is like a **cactus**. Other kinds of cactus plants are shaped like barrels, poles, and flat pads.

Cactus plants are well adapted to desert life. Their roots soak up any drops of rain. They store the water in their fat stems. Waxy skin keeps water inside. Cacti often do not have any leaves because leaves let water escape into the air. Most cactus plants have lots of sharp spines so animals won't eat them. The spines also provide a little shade for the cactus.

Other desert plants also have ways to survive dry periods. When the soil is moist, flowers grow and bloom quickly. Their seeds fall to the ground. Then the seeds wait for the next rainfall. Some may have to wait for years!

The saguaro cactus can live up to 200 years. It doesn't start growing arms until it's around 65 years old.

6

Did you know?

Camels can go for months without a drink. Also, their humps store fat, not water.

Good nesting places are hard to find, so the Gila woodpecker pecks a nest hole in a cactus.

Staying Cool

If you want to see desert animals, you must go in the evening. That is when most desert animals come out to hunt for food. During the day, they try to stay out of the hot sun. They rest in the shade or hide in **burrows** in the ground.

Desert animals have other ways to stay cool. Most have pale skin or fur that reflects the sun's heat. Some have long legs to lift their bodies above the hot sand.

Desert animals can't drink water whenever they want. Instead, most get the water they need from the food they eat.

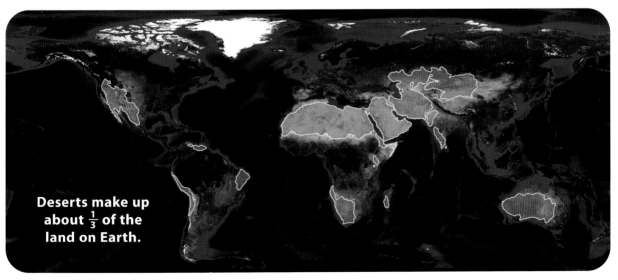

Deserts make up about $\frac{1}{3}$ of the land on Earth.

7

Grasslands

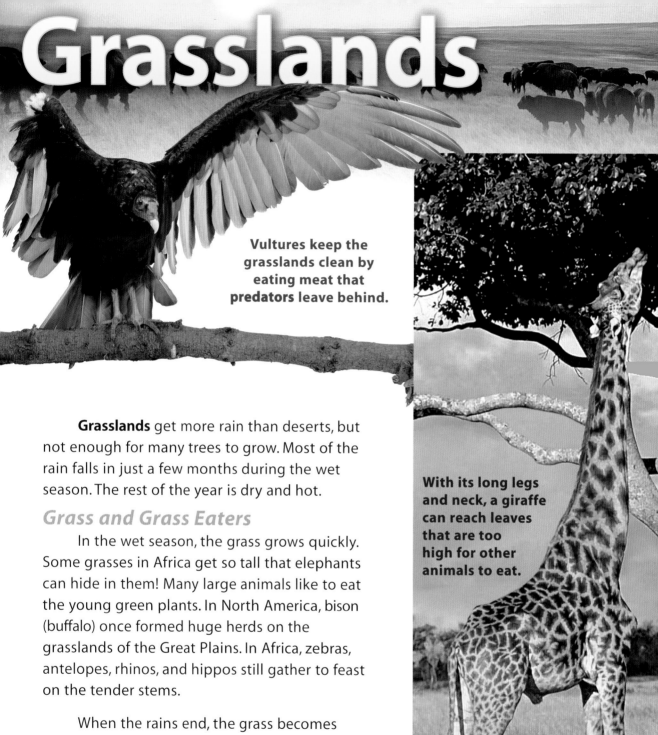

Vultures keep the grasslands clean by eating meat that predators leave behind.

With its long legs and neck, a giraffe can reach leaves that are too high for other animals to eat.

Grasslands get more rain than deserts, but not enough for many trees to grow. Most of the rain falls in just a few months during the wet season. The rest of the year is dry and hot.

Grass and Grass Eaters

In the wet season, the grass grows quickly. Some grasses in Africa get so tall that elephants can hide in them! Many large animals like to eat the young green plants. In North America, bison (buffalo) once formed huge herds on the grasslands of the Great Plains. In Africa, zebras, antelopes, rhinos, and hippos still gather to feast on the tender stems.

When the rains end, the grass becomes yellow and dry. Streams and ponds get smaller or dry up entirely. Now food and water are harder to find. The **herbivores**, or plant-eating animals, must walk many miles to get enough to eat and drink.

A lion's golden coat is hard to see in the dry grass.

Hunters in the Grass

In the dry season, life is hard for herbivores. But it is a little better for the **carnivores**, or meat-eating animals. Hunters such as lions and hyenas wait by the few remaining watering holes. They know that other animals must come to drink, so dinner will be easy to catch.

Staying Safe

In the grasslands, a big challenge is how not to be eaten. The few trees that grow here often have long, sharp thorns. Animals have also adapted in different ways. Some, like antelopes and ostriches, can run very fast. Others, like zebras and giraffes, have bold stripes or spots. This makes it hard for carnivores to pick one animal out of the herd. Large animals like elephants and bison stay safe because they are too big to attack.

Grassland plants and animals face another challenge—their homes are disappearing. Grasslands are often good places to grow crops. The grasslands of North America are mostly farmlands now, and most of the bison are gone. In Africa, grasslands have also been cleared for farms and ranches. Now people all over the world are working to save the grasslands that remain.

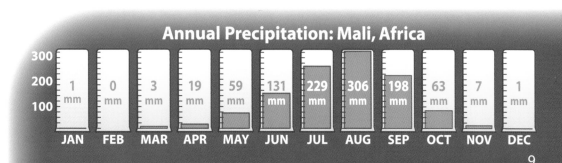

Annual Precipitation: Mali, Africa

	JAN	FEB	MAR	APR	MAY	JUN	JUL	AUG	SEP	OCT	NOV	DEC
mm	1	0	3	19	59	131	229	306	198	63	7	1

Temperate Forests

Have you ever been hiking in a forest in North America? You may have walked beneath tall, shady trees such as oaks, maples, and pines. You might have seen ferns or mushrooms growing beside the trail and wildflowers in the clearings. Perhaps you spotted animals like woodpeckers, deer, or even a bear. If so, you were hiking in a **temperate forest**.

Changes in the Weather

Temperate forests are mostly found in North America, Europe, and northern Asia. They grow in places that have four different seasons: a cold winter, a hot summer, a warm spring, and a cool autumn.

Precipitation such as rain or snow can fall anytime during the year. To live in a temperate forest, plants and animals must be able to adapt to the changing weather.

Woodpeckers peck holes in trees to catch insects that live under the bark.

spring

fall

How Trees Adapt

Some of the trees that grow in temperate forests are **coniferous**. These trees usually keep their leaves all year long. Most of the trees are **deciduous**. This means they lose their leaves for part of the year. New leaves grow in the spring as the weather warms up. In the summer, the leaves use sunlight to make food for the tree. Autumn's cooler temperatures make the leaves lose their green color and turn beautiful shades of red, yellow, and orange. By the time the winter snow arrives, most of the leaves are gone. The tree won't be harmed by the cold.

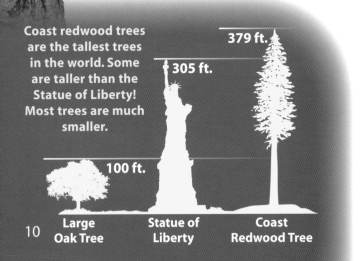

Coast redwood trees are the tallest trees in the world. Some are taller than the Statue of Liberty! Most trees are much smaller.

379 ft.

305 ft.

100 ft.

Large Oak Tree

Statue of Liberty

Coast Redwood Tree

summer

winter

Deciduous trees change with the seasons.

Did you know?

Mushrooms are a type of fungus. They get food from dead leaves and wood on the forest floor.

Flying South

Animals in temperate forests must also survive the changing weather. Some simply leave when the weather turns cold. In the winter, many birds and even butterflies **migrate**, making long flights to warmer places.

A Long Sleep

Other animals solve the problem with **hibernation**, or sleeping through the winter. Sleeping uses very little energy, so the animals don't need to eat much food during this time. You probably know that bears sleep through cold weather. But did you know that some frogs, bats, and even snakes spend their winters dreaming in hidden places?

Bears eat fish, berries, and many other foods. They must build up their fat before the snow falls.

11

Tropical Rain Forests

The toucan uses its large, colorful beak to crack nuts and get food.

Over half of all the different kinds of plants and animals in the world live in one special environment: the **rain forest**. Tropical rain forests are found near the **equator**, an imaginary line that circles the earth halfway between the North and South Poles. Here, the weather is hot and steamy all year long. Rain falls almost every day.

With so much heat and water, rain forests are full of life. Many different plants and animals compete for food, space, and light. They try to get as much of what they need as they can.

Living in Layers

A rain forest grows in four different layers. Each layer is home to its own group of plants and animals that have adapted to it.

Towering above all other trees, a few taller trees rise up to catch the sunlight. They form the **emergent layer**.

Next, rain forest trees crowd together, and their branches mix to create a green "roof" that shades the plants and animals under it. This layer is called the **canopy**.

Below the canopy is the **understory**. This is where you'll find flowers and fruit. Ferns, orchids, and vines also grow on the branches.

The bottom layer is the **forest floor**. It is covered with dead leaves that have dropped from above. Very little sunlight reaches it, so few plants grow here.

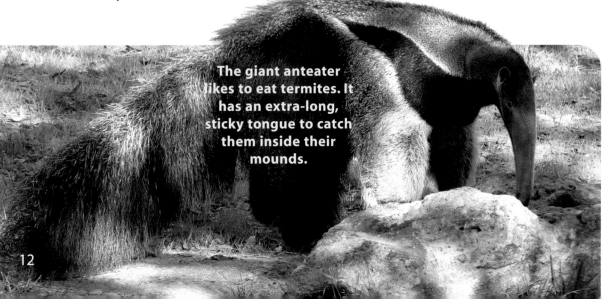

The giant anteater likes to eat termites. It has an extra-long, sticky tongue to catch them inside their mounds.

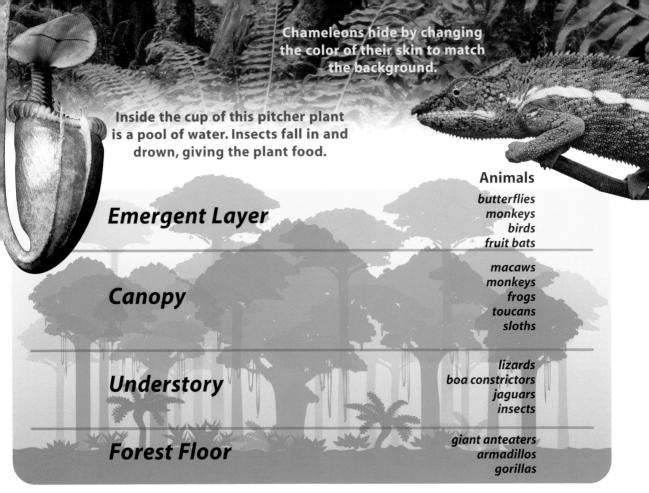

Chameleons hide by changing the color of their skin to match the background.

Inside the cup of this pitcher plant is a pool of water. Insects fall in and drown, giving the plant food.

Animals

Emergent Layer
*butterflies
monkeys
birds
fruit bats*

Canopy
*macaws
monkeys
frogs
toucans
sloths*

Understory
*lizards
boa constrictors
jaguars
insects*

Forest Floor
*giant anteaters
armadillos
gorillas*

Fighting for Food

While rain forest plants compete for space and sunlight, the animals compete for food. Brightly colored birds fly through the canopy, eating seeds and fruit. Monkeys are looking for seeds and fruit, too. They swing through the branches, moving to different trees as the fruit gets ripe. At the same time, eagles, leopards, and snakes are hunting for the birds and monkeys.

On the forest floor, ants, termites, and other insects eat leaves and wood—and each other. Anteaters and frogs snack on the insects. Huge snakes called pythons hide in the leaves, waiting to surprise any careless animal that walks by.

Finding Mates

Another challenge for animals is finding mates so they can reproduce. With so many different animals, it can be hard to find another of your own kind! Bright colors and loud calls are two ways rain forest animals have adapted to meet this challenge.

Did you know?

This frog's bright color warns other animals that it is poisonous to eat.

13

Wetlands

Wetlands are "in-between" places. They are found in between deep water and dry land, such as along the coast or near lakes and rivers.

Many Kinds of Wetlands

There are many different kinds of wetlands. Swamps and marshes are two of them. Some wetlands are covered with shallow water all the time. Others only have water when they are flooded by rain or when the ocean tides are high.

Wetlands on the coast have salt water, while inland wetlands have freshwater. Where rivers flow into the sea, freshwater and salt water mix to form another kind of wetland. Different kinds of plants and animals live in each type of wetland.

An alligator is a fearsome hunter. Nostrils on the top of its snout let it hide itself just below the surface of a river or pool of water.

Challenges for Plants

Plants that live in wetlands must adapt to their watery environment. They must find ways to hang on to the soft mud, or they will be washed away by moving water. They must be able to rise above the water to get light and oxygen.

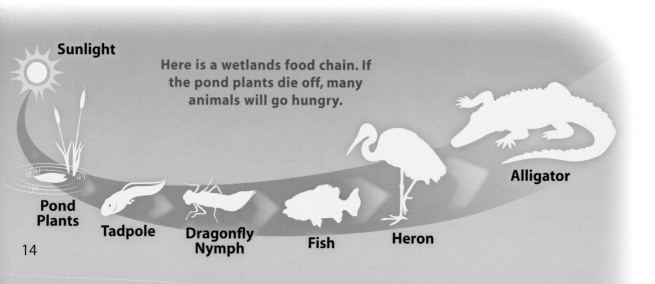

Sunlight

Here is a wetlands food chain. If the pond plants die off, many animals will go hungry.

Pond Plants

Tadpole

Dragonfly Nymph

Fish

Heron

Alligator

Mangroves are able to grow in salty water. Their stilt-like roots hold them upright.

Dragonflies lay their eggs underwater. Young dragonflies, called nymphs, live underwater for many years. They hunt tadpoles and small fish.

In the Water and on the Land

Many wetland animals live both in water and on dry land in their environment. **Amphibians** like frogs and salamanders are well adapted for wetlands. They lay their eggs in or near water. When the eggs hatch, the babies swim like fish and breathe through gills. As adults, they move to dry land and breathe air. Some insects, such as dragonflies, also spend a part of their lives underwater.

Birds in the Wetlands

With all the plants, snails, insects, and fish to eat, wetlands are good places for birds. Some birds live there all year. Others stop to eat and rest on their way to other places.

Wetland birds often have long legs. This helps them stand in the shallow water and look down to find food. Their bills are shaped for the kinds of food they eat. Sharp bills spear or grab fish. Spoon-shaped bills can scoop up and filter out mud to get to the small animals.

The heron's long legs let it wade in the water to look for frogs and fish. When it spots one, it grabs it with its sharp bill.

Oceans

Oceans have many **habitats**, or places where different plants and animals live. There are warm coral reefs, shallow waters, deep canyons, and wide-open seas. Different kinds of plants and animals live in each one.

Coral Reefs

You might think a **coral reef** is a garden of underwater plants. But most of those "plants" are really animals! Coral animals are very tiny. Their skeletons form fans, branches, and many other shapes. After thousands of years, the coral can build up into a reef or even an island!

This "plant" and "brain" is really a group of animals called coral.

Hiding in the Open Ocean

How can you hide in the open ocean? One way is to match the background. Animals in open-ocean habitats often have dark backs and pale bellies. Seen from below, their bellies match the sky. Seen from above, they match the dark, deep water below them.

Did you know?

Dolphins are mammals, not fish. A dolphin breathes air through the nostril on top of its head.

Like dolphins, sharks are fast-swimming hunters. That is why they have similar body shapes. They have adapted to move quickly through the ocean.

Coastal Waters

Water near the surface gets lots of sunlight, so **plankton** are plentiful. Plankton are very tiny plants and animals that float in the water. Many small fish enjoy this seafood soup—and many other animals enjoy the small fish! Crabs and lobsters catch their food with their big claws. Octopuses use the suckers on their long arms to grab and hold the animals they eat. Flower-like animals called **sea anemones** (uh-NEH-muh-neez) trap food with their "petals." Jellyfish drift through the water, dragging long, stinging **tentacles** behind them.

Open Oceans

In the open ocean, fast-swimming hunters like dolphins and sharks search for fish to eat. The fish protect themselves by forming big groups called schools.

Deep Seas

No ray of sunlight can reach the deepest parts of the ocean. Some animals adapt to the darkness by making their own light!

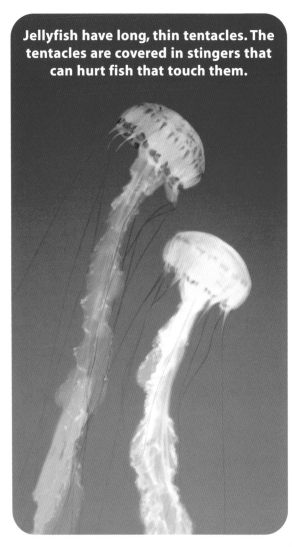

Jellyfish have long, thin tentacles. The tentacles are covered in stingers that can hurt fish that touch them.

Polar Regions

Polar regions are the areas close to the Earth's poles. The region in the north is called the **Arctic**. In the south is the continent of **Antarctica**. In both regions, the land and water are covered by ice most of the year. Even though the sun never sets in the summer, it does not get hot.

Oceans of Life

The biggest challenges for living things are staying warm and finding food. That is why most life in the polar regions is found in the ocean! The water is very cold, but the temperature does not change as much as it does on land. This makes it easier for animals to adapt to it.

The Tundra

The Arctic Ocean takes up the biggest part of the Arctic region. It is mostly covered by ice all year. The frozen land around the ocean is called the **tundra**. When some of the ice on the tundra melts in the summer, large herds of **caribou** come to feed on the plants. Thousands of birds fly in. Foxes and wolves come to the tundra to hunt the other animals.

Antarctica

There are almost no plants on the frozen continent of Antarctica, and no animals can live there all year—except penguins! Penguins have adapted to

Millions of tiny animals called krill live in the Arctic Ocean. They are a favorite food of whales, like this humpback.

Each spring, caribou, also called reindeer, walk hundreds of miles to get to the tundra.

survive the terrible winter storms. There is no food on the land, so they hunt for fish in the ocean. They have feathers and thick fat, called blubber, to keep them warm. Penguins have even found a way to keep eggs and chicks warm on the ice. They cuddle them on top of their feet!

Melting Ice

In the Arctic, ice covers part of the ocean and land all year. But scientists say that more of the ice melts every summer. This makes life harder for polar bears, which live and hunt on the ice. If all of the summer ice disappears, polar bears may also disappear—forever.

Penguins cannot fly—but they swim very well. They use their wings as flippers and steer with their feet.

Summer 1979	Summer 2003

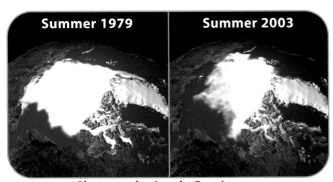

Changes in Arctic Sea Ice

Did you know?

You won't find penguins and polar bears together, except in a zoo—or a movie! Polar bears live near the North Pole, but penguins only live south of the equator.

19

Challenges and Adaptations

Environments	Challenges
Deserts	staying cool
	getting water
Grasslands	finding food
Temperate Forests	cold winters
Tropical Rain Forests	competition
	finding mates
Wetlands	shallow water
Oceans	staying safe
	catching food
Polar Regions	staying warm
	finding food

Living Things   # Adaptations

jackrabbits . . . . large ears release heat
kangaroo rats . . . . get water from seeds
cacti . . . . water is stored in fat, waxy stems

herd animals . . . . able to walk long distances
carnivores . . . . wait by watering holes

deciduous trees . . . . lose leaves every winter
bats . . . . sleep in caves
birds . . . . migrate to warmer places

plants and animals . . . . live in their own layers
birds and frogs . . . . loud songs or calls

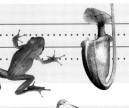

mangroves . . . . stilt-like roots
herons . . . . long legs

dolphins . . . . light-colored bellies match sky
fish . . . . swim in large groups
sharks . . . . slim bodies for speed
jellyfish . . . . tentacles with stingers

penguins . . . . layers of feathers and fat
polar bears . . . . layers of fat; thick fur
penguins . . . . able to travel long distances
caribou . . . . can smell plants under snow

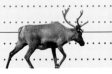

Glossary

adapt.....................................to change to fit the environment

amphibians........................animals that live in water and on land, such as frogs and salamanders

Antarctica..........................continent around the South Pole

Arctic...................................area near the North Pole

burrow.................................hole or tunnel made by an animal

cactus..................................desert plant with spines and a thick stem

canopy.................................rain forest layer with many treetops close together

caribou................................large deer, also called reindeer

carnivore.............................meat-eating animal

coniferous trees...............trees that usually keep their leaves all year long

coral reef.............................rocky ocean habitat made from the skeletons of coral animals

deciduous trees................trees that lose leaves during one season each year

desert...................................dry region that gets very little rainfall

emergent layer.................top layer of a rain forest

environment.....................natural place where plants and animals live

equator...............................imaginary line that circles the earth halfway between the poles

forest floor	bottom layer of a rain forest
grasslands	open land covered with grass, such as meadows and prairies
habitat	place where plants and animals live
herbivore	plant-eating animal
hibernation	sleeping through the winter
migrate	to move to a different place when the weather changes
oxygen	air needed by plants and animals to survive
plankton	tiny plants and animals that float near the surface of the ocean
polar regions	areas around the North and South Poles
precipitation	water that falls from the sky, such as rain or snow
predators	animals that eat other animals
rain forest	hot, damp forest habitat found near the equator
reproduce	to lay eggs, have babies, or make seeds
sea anemone	flower-like sea animal
temperate forest	environment with four different seasons
tentacles	long, thin body parts of a jellyfish that sting
tundra	frozen land in the Arctic region
understory	rain forest layer below the canopy
wetlands	wet areas in between deep water and dry land

Index